Amazing life cycles
MAMMALS
by Honor Head

Copyright © ticktock Entertainment Ltd 2007

First published in Great Britain in 2007 by ticktock Media Ltd,
The Old Sawmill, Goods Station Road, Tunbridge Wells, Kent, TN1 2DP

ticktock project editor: Ruth Owen
ticktock project designer: Sara Greasley
With thanks to: Sally Morgan, Jean Coppendale and Elizabeth Wiggans

ISBN 978-1-84696-070-3 pbk

Printed in China
9 8 7 6 5 4

Picture credits (t=top; b=bottom; c=centre; l=left; r=right):
Ardea: 28c. Corbis: 20 main, 21t, 31t. FLPA: 5t, 7b, 9tr, 9tl, 13 main, 15cl, 16tl, 16c, 21b, 24c, 26 main.
Nature Picture Library: 16–17 main. NHPA: 30b. Oxford Scientific Photo Library: 10 main, 17t, 18c.
Shutterstock: OFC, 1, 2, 3, 4tl, 4tr, 5b, 6t, 7t, 8tl, 10tl, 11t, 11b, 12tl, 12 main, 13t, 14tl, 14tr, 14cl, 14b, 14–15c, 15tl, 15tr, 15cr, 15b,
20tl, 22tl, 23t, 23 main, 24tl, 24–25 main, 25t, 26tl, 27t, 27b, 28tl, 29b, 30tl, 31 main, OBC.
Superstock: 4l, 9 main, 18tl, 18–19 main, 22b, 30c. Terry Hardie – www.orcaresearch.org: 8 main.
ticktock image archive: map page 6. Wendy Blanshard, Australian Koala Foundation, www.savethekoala.com: 29t.
Every effort has been made to trace copyright holders, and we apologise in advance for any omissions. We would be
pleased to insert the appropriate acknowledgments in any subsequent edition of this publication.

Contents

Words that look **bold like this** are in the glossary.

What is a mammal?

This hairy cow is a mammal.

A mammal is an animal that feeds its babies with milk. Mammals are also **endothermic**. This means their body **temperature** stays about the same no matter how hot or cold the air or water is around them.

Most mammals give birth to live babies. When a mammal baby is born the mother feeds it with milk from inside her body. This is called suckling.

A hairy hippo nose!

Mammals also have hair on their bodies. A hippopotamus is a mammal with smooth skin, but it has hair in its ears and on its nose.

The leopard cubs in this picture are suckling from their mother.

This pipistrelle bat is sitting on a scientist's finger while he studies it.

Mammals can be tiny like a pipistrelle bat, or enormous like an elephant!

Did you know that people are mammals, too?

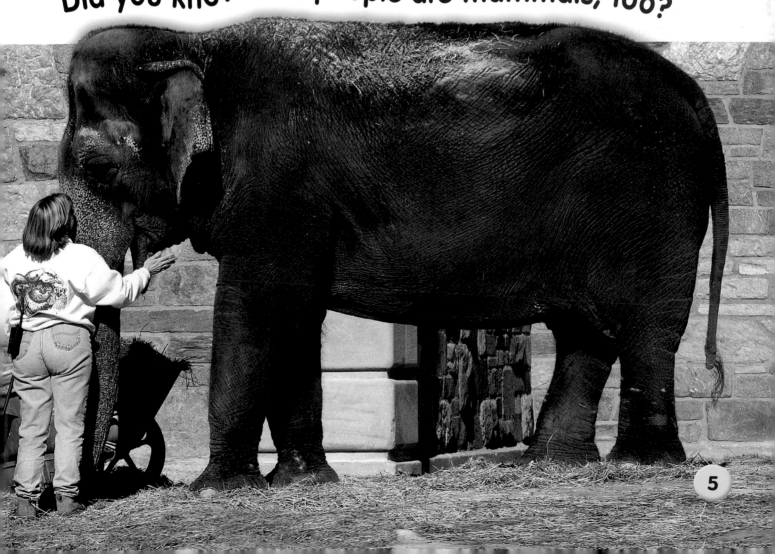

Mammal habitats

Polar bears are mammals that live in the icy, snowy Arctic.

A habitat is the place where a plant or an animal lives. Mammals live in hot **desert** habitats and cold, icy places, such as the Arctic. The sea is a habitat. Mammals such as whales and seals live in this habitat.

Mammals live in most of the world's habitats.

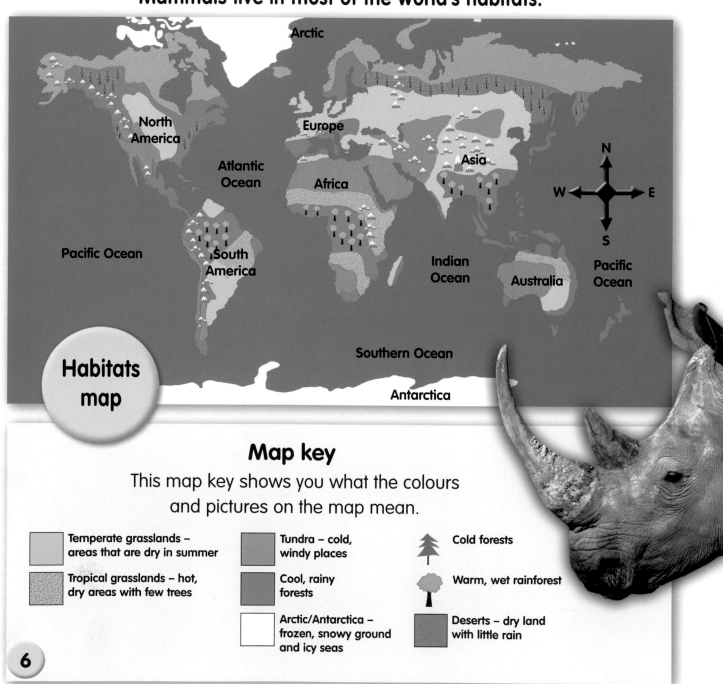

Arctic

North America

Europe

Asia

Atlantic Ocean

Africa

Pacific Ocean

South America

Indian Ocean

Australia

Pacific Ocean

Southern Ocean

Antarctica

N
W — E
S

Habitats map

Map key
This map key shows you what the colours and pictures on the map mean.

Temperate grasslands – areas that are dry in summer

Tropical grasslands – hot, dry areas with few trees

Arctic/Antarctica – frozen, snowy ground and icy seas

Tundra – cold, windy places

Cool, rainy forests

Cold forests

Warm, wet rainforest

Deserts – dry land with little rain

Rainforests are warm, wet habitats with lots of trees and plants. Mammals such as monkeys, gorillas and sloths live here.

Grasslands are hot, dry habitats. Mammals such as rhinos, elephants, giraffes and meerkats live on the grasslands in Africa.

Sloths hang upside down – the baby rides on mum's chest.

The rhino calf in this picture is suckling from his mother.

AMAZING MAMMAL FACT
Many African grassland mammals, such as lions, sleep during the day and hunt at night when it is cool.

Meat-eating mammals

Animals that eat meat are **carnivores**. Most carnivore mammals have sharp claws and teeth to help them catch and eat their **prey**. Animals that hunt are called **predators**.

Big cats such as tigers and cheetahs are carnivores.

AMAZING MAMMAL FACT
Orcas are also called killer whales because they kill and eat seals, penguins and other whales.

Sometimes orcas surf onto a beach to catch their prey. The waves then pull them back out to sea.

The giant anteater uses its long, sharp claws to tear a hole in a **termite** or ant nest. It puts its long, sticky tongue in the hole and scoops up the bugs.

A termite nest

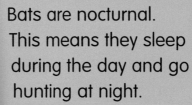

Bats are nocturnal. This means they sleep during the day and go hunting at night.

This pipistrelle bat is hunting a moth.

Meerkats have sharp claws so they can dig for food such as worms.

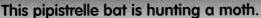
Meerkats chase and catch scorpions and lizards.

Before the meerkat eats the **scorpion**, it bites off its sting!

Plant-eating mammals

A koala has a home tree where it lives.

Animals which only eat plants are called **herbivores**. They eat leaves, roots, fruit or flowers.
Some herbivore mammals have developed special ways to help them eat the food they need.

Hippos live in Africa. In the day they keep cool in rivers. They come out of the river at sunset to eat grass during the night.

AMAZING MAMMAL FACT
Hippos use their wide lips to grab grass. Then they swing their heads from side to side to pull up the grass from the roots.

Koalas only eat one type of food – the leaves of the eucalyptus tree. These trees grow in Australia where koalas live.

Koalas spend their time eating and sleeping in the eucalyptus trees.

Warthogs use their strong snouts to dig up the hard ground to find tasty underground roots.

Warthogs live on African grasslands.

11

Mum meets dad

Some mammals **mate** and then the male and female bring up their young together. Other mammals meet, mate and then the female is left to look after the babies alone or with other females in a group.

Koala dads don't help care for their babies.

A male and a female meerkat will become a couple. They lead a family group and are the only ones in the group allowed to have babies.

AMAZING MAMMAL FACT
Meerkats live in big family groups of about 40 animals.

When a male and female warthog have mated, the male leaves. Adult male warthogs live on their own.

Male warthogs fight over who gets to mate with a female.

When a male orca is grown-up and ready to mate, he goes to another pod and mates with a female. Then he goes back to live with his mother in his family group. Female orcas bring up their babies in their family group.

The orca couple swim around each other – it's like dancing!

What is a life cycle?

A life cycle is all the different **stages** and changes that an animal or plant goes through in its life. This diagram shows a mammal life cycle.

A baby lion is called a cub.

1 A female mammal gives birth to a live baby or babies.

This is the life cycle of a lion.

6 When they become adults, male and female mammals meet and mate.

5 Some mammals live with their family group when they grow up. Some go off and live on their own.

Amazing mammal life cycles

An orca

In this book we are going to find out about some amazing mammal life cycles – from orcas who live in the sea, to treetop koalas.

A koala

2

Female mammals feed their babies milk.

Lions are meat-eaters.

3

Mammal mothers look after their babies. Sometimes the fathers help, too.

4

Mammals teach their babies how to hunt, or find food. Young meat-eaters practise their hunting skills on each other.

Father bats do not help
look after the babies.

Pipistrelle bats

Pipistrelle bats usually have one baby each year.
Hundreds of female bats gather together to give
birth in a building such as a church or barn.
Sometimes they gather under a bridge or in a cave.

Bat pup

Mother bat

A baby bat is called a pup.
When the pups are born
the mothers and pups stay
together in a huge group
called a nursery roost.

**LIFE CYCLE
FACTS**

A pipistrelle bat is
pregnant for about 50 days.
A female starts to have
babies when she is
between 6 and 12
months old.

16

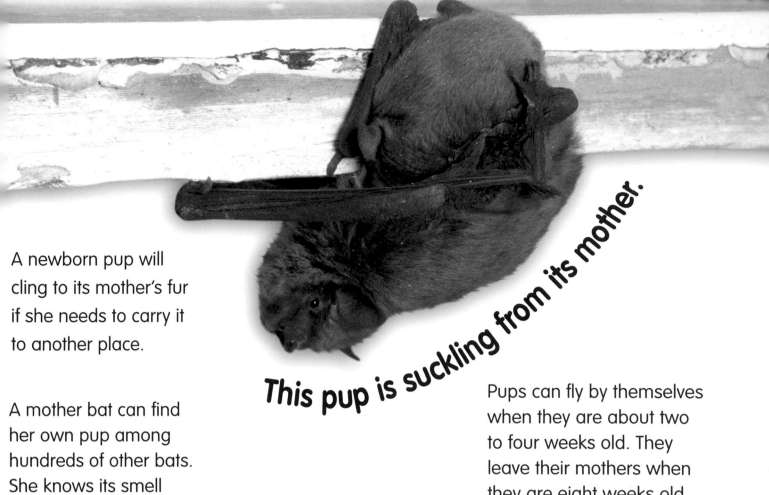

A newborn pup will cling to its mother's fur if she needs to carry it to another place.

A mother bat can find her own pup among hundreds of other bats. She knows its smell and its sound.

This pup is suckling from its mother.

Pups can fly by themselves when they are about two to four weeks old. They leave their mothers when they are eight weeks old.

This picture shows bats in a nursery roost.

Giant anteaters

Giant anteaters live on hot, dry grasslands in South America. Adult giant anteaters live alone. When the male and female have mated, the male leaves.

An anteater's claws grow to 10 centimetres long.

An anteater can use its tail for support like a third leg.

The female giant anteater gives birth standing up on her back legs.

AMAZING MAMMAL FACT

The baby anteater is born with fur and sharp claws. It crawls onto its mother's back where she licks it clean. Baby anteaters suckle for about six months.

After a few months the baby hops off its mother's back to explore and then hops on again.

The baby stays with its mother until it is grown-up, at the age of about two years.

If the baby falls off, it grunts to let mum know.

Orcas

Orca babies, called calves, are born underwater. They are born tail first. An orca calf can be 2.4 metres long when it is born!

A newborn orca weighs 180 kilograms.

LIFE CYCLE FACTS

Orcas are pregnant for 15 to 18 months. Females start to have babies when they are about 15 years old.

As soon as the calf is born the mother pushes the baby to the surface so that it can take its first breath of air.

The mother orca guides the calf to the surface of the water using her flippers and her nose.

Calf

Flipper

An orca calf feeds on its mother's milk for the first one to two years of its life.

The mother orca teaches the calf how to hunt and catch food.

Most orca pods have about 30 members.

Orca families talk to each other using grunts, whistles and squeals. Calves learn how to make these noises.

Meerkats

Meerkats live in groups that include males, females and babies, called kits. They live in **burrows** under the ground.

The meerkat's dark eye rings protect its eyes from the bright sun.

LIFE CYCLE FACTS

Meerkats are pregnant for 75 days. A female starts to have babies when she is one year old.

Newborn kits are helpless and do not have hair. They are born in the burrow and stay there until they are about three to four weeks old.

Female meerkats have three to five babies at one time.

22

Adult meerkats take it in turns to babysit while others go out hunting.

Meerkats stand up on their back legs to keep a look out for predators such as eagles.

When the kits are about one month old, they start to go on hunting trips. Each kit has its own adult that teaches it how to hunt.

Warthogs

The female warthog gives birth to two or three babies at one time in an underground burrow. The babies, or piglets, leave the burrow when they are about two weeks old.

Warthogs use their good sense of smell to find food.

It is important that the newborn piglets do not get wet or cold. They sleep on a raised shelf at the back of the burrow to make sure they stay dry.

Adult warthogs and older piglets enjoy a mud bath to cool off on a hot day.

Warthogs use their sharp **tusks** to fight off predators such as lions. Both male and female warthogs have tusks.

Warthog piglets are not born with tusks. The tusks grow as the baby grows.

LIFE CYCLE FACTS

Warthogs are pregnant for 6 months. A female starts to have babies when she is 18 months old.

The piglets suckle for about four months. Male piglets stay with their mother for about two years. Females go off on their own when they are about 18 months old.

Hippopotamuses

Male hippos fight over females.

Hippos live in a group called a herd. The herd includes one adult male, lots of females and their young. When a female is ready to give birth, she looks for a soft place at the edge of the river.

The hippo baby, or calf, is born in shallow water at the edge of the river. The mother quickly pushes the baby to the surface so that it can breathe.

LIFE CYCLE FACTS

Hippos are pregnant for 8 months. A female starts to have babies when she is 9 years old.

The mother and calf move away from the herd for the first couple of weeks. This stops the baby being hurt by accident by one of the other adults.

An adult hippo can weigh 1.5 tonnes!

Most grown-up hippos stay in the herd where they were born. A male hippo may start his own herd when he is about 20 years old.

AMAZING MAMMAL FACT
Sometimes a hippo calf will rest on its mother's back. It will slip into the water if it gets too hot and then climb back on.

The female koala gives birth in the eucalyptus trees.

Koalas

Koalas are marsupials. This means that the mother has a pouch on her tummy where her baby lives. The pouch is a bit like a pocket. A newborn koala is called a joey.

LIFE CYCLE FACTS

Koalas are pregnant for 35 days. A female starts to have babies when she is 2 years old.

This newborn joey is about the size of a jellybean.

The newborn joey is tiny! It has no hair, ears or eyes. It crawls into its mother's pouch. In the pouch the joey drinks its mother's milk.

The joey's fur, ears and eyes grow. The joey gets bigger and bigger. When the joey is about six to seven months old it starts to ride on its mother's back.

Joey

At about one year old the koala leaves its mother. This is usually when the mother gives birth to another joey.

That's amazing!

All mammal mums care for their babies. They feed them milk and teach them how to find food. But mammal babies begin life in lots of different ways!

A baby giraffe is called a calf.

Female polar bears go to sleep in a den for the winter. While they are in the den they give birth to their babies, called cubs.

The polar bear's den is under the snow. Can you see the cub?

AMAZING MAMMAL FACT

The newborn polar bear cubs are about 30 centimetres long. They are blind, pink and hairless.

The mother and cubs leave the den after four or five months when it is spring.

The female platypus lays two or three grape-size eggs. The eggs **hatch** about 12 days later. The baby platypuses drink milk from their mother.

The giraffe is the world's tallest animal mum. The female gives birth standing up. The giraffe calf drops two metres to the ground!

A newborn giraffe is 1.8 metres tall!

Glossary

burrows – Tunnels and holes under the ground where some animals live.

carnivores – Animals which eat meat. These animals are also predators.

desert – A place where it hardly ever rains. Deserts can be very hot in the day. Some deserts get cold at night.

endothermic – Animals whose body temperature stays the same no matter how hot or cold the air or water is around them. You are endothermic!

hatch – When a baby bird or animal breaks out of its egg. It is like being born.

herbivores – Animals which do not eat meat. Herbivores eat foods such as grass, leaves, fruits and flowers.

mate – When a male and female animal meet and have babies.

predators – Animals which hunt and kill other animals for food.

prey – Animals which are hunted by other animals as food.

scorpion – A Small animal with eight legs, two arms with big claws, and a tail with a poisonous sting.

stages – Different times of an animal's life when the animal changes in some way.

temperature – How hot or cold something is.

termite – An insect which is like a large ant. Termites live in big groups.

tusks – Long, sharp pointed teeth.

Index